# LO QUE HACEN LOS TRABAJADORES SANITARIOS

## WHAT SANITATION WORKERS DO

What Does a Community Helper Do? Bilingual

Heather Miller

# Words to Know

**Dumpster**—Large container used to hold garbage.

**garbage**—Food and other things that are thrown out.

**refrigerator**—A device that keeps food cold.

**sanitation**—Keeping things free of unhealthy things, like trash or germs.

# Palabras a conocer

**la basura**— Alimentos y otras cosas que se botan.

**el contenedor de basura**— Recipiente grande usado para contener la basura.

**el refrigerador**— Aparato que mantiene los alimentos fríos.

**la sanidad**— Mantener las cosas sin elementos insalubres, como deshechos o gérmenes.

## Enslow Elementary

an imprint of

**Enslow Publishers, Inc.**

40 Industrial Road
Box 398
Berkeley Heights, NJ 07922
USA

http://www.enslow.com

# Contents/Contenido

**Sanitation** workers drive **garbage** trucks.

**Los** trabajadores sanitarios conducen camiones de **basura**.

# Garbage Day!

The street is quiet. It is still dark. Suddenly, RUMBLE, RUMBLE, RUMBLE! A big garbage truck drives down the road. It is garbage day in your neighborhood. There is a lot of trash!

• • • • • • • • • • • • • • • • • • • • • • • • • • •

# ¡Dia de recogida de basura!

La calle está tranquila. Todavía es de noche. De pronto, ¡RUMBLE, RUMBLE, RUMBLE! Un gran camión de basura viene por la calle. Es el día de recogida de basura en tu vecindario. Hay muchos deshechos.

Sanitation workers even clean up the streets of big cities.

Los trabajadores sanitarios limpian incluso las calles de las grandes ciudades.

# Working in All Types of Weather

Sanitation workers work in all types of weather. They work in the hot sun. They work in cold snow. In rain, ice, or wind, sanitation workers must work to pick up the trash.

• • • • • • • • • • • • • • • • • • • • • • • • • • • •

# Trabajando bajo cualquier condición del tiempo

Los trabajadores sanitarios trabajan bajo cualquier condición del tiempo. Ellos trabajan bajo un sol ardiente. Ellos trabajan bajo la fría nieve. Bajo la lluvia, el hielo o el viento, los trabajadores sanitarios tienen que trabajar para recoger los deshechos.

Piles of trash on curbs are picked up by sanitation workers.

Montones de deshechos son recogidos en los bordes de las aceras por los trabajadores sanitarios.

# Where Do Sanitation Workers Stop for Trash?

Sanitation workers stop at many places to pick up garbage. They drive through neighborhoods and stop at each house as they go. They empty **Dumpsters** by stores, diners, shopping centers, and hospitals.

• • • • • • • • • • • • • • • • • • • • • • • • • • • •

# ¿Dónde se detienen a recoger deshechos los trabajadores sanitarios?

Los trabajadores sanitarios se detienen en muchos lugares para colectar la basura. Ellos conducen por muchos vecindarios y de camino paran en cada casa. Ellos vacían los **contenedores de basura** que están junto a las tiendas, los restaurantes, los centros comerciales y los hospitales.

Sanitation workers lift heavy bags of trash into their trucks.

Los trabajadores sanitarios levantan bolsas pesadas de deshechos a sus camiones.

# Picking Up Trash

Sanitation workers must be strong. They lift many heavy things. They carry garbage cans, boxes, and bags filled with trash. Sometimes, they even lift **refrigerators**!

• • • • • • • • • • • • • • • • • • • • • • • • • • • • •

# Recogiendo los deshechos

Los trabajadores sanitarios deben ser fuertes. Ellos levantan muchas cosas pesadas. Ellos cargan botes de basura, cajas y bolsas llenas de deshechos. ¡Algunas veces ellos cargan hasta **refrigeradores**!

Sanitation workers work together. In this small town in Vermont, trash is picked up and loaded onto a cart pulled by a horse.

Los trabajadores sanitarios trabajan unidos. En esta pequeña ciudad de Vermont, la basura se recoge y se carga en una carreta tirada por caballo.

# Staying Safe

Sanitation workers must be careful when they work. Garbage can be slippery or sharp. Sanitation workers work together. They help keep one another safe.

• • • • • • • • • • • • • • • • • • • • • • • • • •

# Mantenerse a salvo

Los trabajadores sanitarios deben ser cuidadosos mientras trabajan. La basura puede ser resbalosa o cortante. Los trabajadores sanitarios trabajan unidos. Ellos se ayudan para mantener su seguridad.

Sanitation workers wear special clothes to keep them safe.

Los trabajadores sanitarios usan ropa especial para mantenerse a salvo.

Thick gloves protect their hands from broken glass, sharp metal, and germs. Bright, colored vests help other drivers see sanitation workers who are working on the road. They even wear special hats to protect them on the job.

● ● ● ● ● ● ● ● ● ● ● ● ● ● ● ● ● ● ● ● ● ● ● ● ● ● ● ● ● ●

Guantes gruesos protegen sus manos de los vidrios rotos, metales cortantes y gérmenes. Los chalecos de brillante color ayudan a que los conductores vean a los trabajadores sanitarios que están trabajando en la calle. Ellos incluso usan sombreros especiales que los protegen en su trabajo.

**Garbage trucks go to the dump. The trucks unload all the trash.**

**Los camiones de basura van al vertedero. Los camiones descargan todos los deshechos.**

# Garbage Trucks

Sanitation workers drive trucks. Some trucks are big. Other trucks are small. Sanitation workers load them with garbage. They take the trucks to the dump when they are full. There, the trash is taken off the truck. Sanitation workers go back to pick up more garbage.

• • • • • • • • • • • • • • • • • • • • • • • • • • • • • • • • • •

# Camiones de basura

Los trabajadores sanitarios conducen camiones. Algunos camiones son grandes. Otros camiones son pequeños. Los trabajadores sanitarios los cargan de basura. Ellos llevan los camiones al vertedero cuando están llenos. Allí, descargan los deshechos de los camiones. Los trabajadores sanitarios regresan a recoger más basura.

Raccoons and other animals hide in Dumpsters. They look for piles of trash. Sanitation workers empty Dumpsters so these animals stay away.

Los mapaches y otros animales se esconden en los contenedores. Ellos buscan los montones de deshechos. Los trabajadores sanitarios vacían los contenedores de basura para que estos animales se mantengan alejados.

# Helping the Community

People throw things away every day. If sanitation workers did not do their jobs, piles of trash would grow and grow.

Garbage is stinky and ugly. It can attract animals like rats and raccoons. These animals are dangerous to people and pets.

# Ayudando a la comunidad

Las personas botan cosas todos los días. Si los trabajadores sanitarios no hicieran su trabajo, los montones de deshechos crecerían y crecerían.

La basura es apestosa y fea. La basura puede atraer animales como ratas y mapaches. Estos animales son dañinos para las personas y las mascotas.

Every day, sanitation workers take garbage to the dump. They help keep our streets clean and safe.

Todos los días los trabajadores sanitarios llevan la basura al vertedero. Ellos mantienen nuestras calles limpias y sanas.

RUMBLE, RUMBLE! The next day, the garbage truck is back on the road. Sanitation workers work almost every day to keep their communities safe and clean. Sanitation workers are community heroes.

• • • • • • • • • • • • • • • • • • • • • • • • • • • • • • • •

¡RUMBLE, RUMBLE! Al día siguiente el camión de basura está nuevamente en la calle. Los trabajadores sanitarios trabajan casi todos los días para mantener sus comunidades sanas y limpias. Los trabajadores sanitarios son héroes de la comunidad.

# Make Less Waste

How can you help make less waste? It is easy!

When you pack a lunch for school:
    Use a reusable lunch box or bag.
    Use containers you can use again.
    Take only what you know you will eat.

When you look for school supplies:
    Try pens and pencils you can refill.
    Try a sturdy backpack or book bag that
    will last a long time.
    Use up paper from the year before.

When you are at home:
    Use scrap paper to write notes.
    Use cloth napkins instead of paper ones.
    Help your family recycle.

# Creando menos desperdicio

¿Cómo puedes tú ayudar a crear menos deshechos? ¡Eso es fácil!

Cuando tú preparas el almuerzo para la escuela:
    Usa una lonchera o bolsa reutilizable.
    Usa recipientes que puedas utilizar nuevamente.
    Lleva sólo lo que sabes que te vas a comer.

Cuando tú busques artículos de uso escolar:
    Trata de usar plumas y lápices que se puedan rellenar.
    Trata de usar una mochila o maleta fuerte que te dure mucho tiempo.
    Termina de usar el papel del año anterior.

Cuando tú estás en la casa:
    Usa papel de deshecho para escribir notas.
    Usa servilletas de tela en lugar de las de papel.
    Ayuda a tu familia a reciclar.

# Learn More / Más para aprender

## Books / Libros

### In English / En inglés

LeBoutillier, Nate. *A Day in the Life of a Garbage Collector.* Mankato, Minn.: Capstone Press, 2005.

Macken, JoAnn Early. *Sanitation Worker.* Milwaukee, Wisc.: Weekly Reader Early Learning Library, 2003.

### In Spanish / En español

Macken, JoAnn Early. *Sanitation Worker / El recogedor de basura.* Milwaukee, Wisc.: Weekly Reader Early Learning Library, 2003.

## Internet Addresses / Direcciones de Internet

### In English / En inglés

Adventures of the Garbage Gremlin
<http://www.epa.gov/epaoswer/non-hw/recycle/gremlin/gremlin.htm>
Visit a dump and learn about recycling with the Garbage Gremlin.

Creating Less Trash at School
<http://www.moea.state.mn.us/campaign/school/index.html>
Learn more about making less trash.

# Index

# Índice

● ● ● ● ● ● ● ● ● ● ● ● ● ● ● ● ● ● ● ● ● ● ● ● ● ● ● ● ● ● ● ● ● ● ● ●

**Note to Teachers and Parents:** The *What Does a Community Helper Do?* series supports curriculum standards for K–4 learning about community services and helpers. The Words to Know section introduces subject-specific vocabulary. Early readers may require help with these new words.

**Series Literacy Consultant:**
Allan A. De Fina, Ph.D.
Past President of the New Jersey Reading Association
Professor, Department of Literacy Education
New Jersey City University

● ● ● ● ● ● ● ● ● ● ● ● ● ● ● ● ● ● ● ● ● ● ● ● ● ● ● ● ● ● ● ● ● ● ● ●

Enslow Elementary, an imprint of Enslow Publishers, Inc.

Enslow Elementary® is a registered trademark of Enslow Publishers, Inc.

Bilingual edition copyright 2008 by Enslow Publishers, Inc. Originally published in English under the title *What Does a Sanitation Worker Do?* © 2005 by Enslow Publishers, Inc. Bilingual edition translated by Eloísa X. Le Riverend, edited by Susana C. Schultz, of Strictly Spanish, LLC.

Copyright © 2008 by Enslow Publishers, Inc.

All rights reserved.

No part of this book may be reproduced by any means without the written permission of the publisher.

**Library of Congress Cataloging-in-Publication Data**

Miller, Heather.
    [What does a sanitation worker do? Spanish & English]
    Lo que hacen los trabajadores sanitarios = What sanitation workers do / Heather Miller. — Bilingual ed.
      p. cm. — (What does a community helper do? Bilingual)
    Includes bibliographical references and index.
    ISBN-13: 978-0-7660-2829-6
    ISBN-10: 0-7660-2829-1
    1. Sanitation workers—Juvenile literature. 2. Refuse and refuse disposal—Juvenile literature. I. Miller, Heather. What does a sanitation worker do? II. Title. III. Title: Que hacen los trabajadores sanitarios. IV. Title: What sanitation workers do.
    HD8039.S257M5518 2007
    363.72023—dc22                    2006021048

Printed in the United States of America

10 9 8 7 6 5 4 3 2 1

**To Our Readers:**

Every effort has been made to locate all copyright holders of material used in this book. If any errors or omissions have occurred, corrections will be made in future editions of this book.

**Illustration Credits:** Associated Press, pp. 4, 6, 8, 10, 12, 16, 18 (bottom), 20; Associated Press, Effingham Daily News, p. 18 (top); Associated Press, The Daily Reflector, p. 14; Hemera Technologies, Inc. 1997–2000, pp. 2, 15, 22 (top); © 2004 JupiterImages, p. 22 (middle and bottom); Punchstock, p. 1.

**Cover Illustration:** Punchstock (bottom); top left to right (photos 1, 2, and 4: Associated Press; photo 3: Associated Press, The Daily Reflector.)